PRAISE FOR
CALM IN THE CHAOS

"This book is like a magic compass pointing the way to a positive impact. Using Stoicism, the authors show readers how to build trust, confidence, and inspiration for what a team can achieve together. Use this book as a framework for great leadership and a map for the journey toward a rich legacy!"

Brad Black, Humanex Ventures President and CEO

"Turbulent times in education require a radical rethinking of leadership tactics. This is a brilliant and practical guide that awakens the masterful concepts of Stoicism and demonstrates their timeless impact on successful organizations."

Jennifer Womble, Conference Chair of FETC

"Filled with powerful quotes and real-world scenarios, this book will fill your mind and heart with the concepts of Stoicism while stretching your own personal and professional core leadership values. It will cause you to not only reflect upon yourself and your work, but it will also leave you with practical ways to lead better, feel more deeply, and ultimately, become a better person. It's a must-read for leaders and their teams looking to engage in reflective dialogue and navigate the complexities of leadership."

Dr. Courtney Orzel, IASA Associate Director of Professional Development

"Being an education leader is one of the greatest responsibilities that can be bestowed upon an individual. These leaders are responsible for shaping students' minds to better the world while also looking out for the needs of staff. On top of that, education leaders face daily challenges, critical decisions, resentment, anger, envy, and much more. In this book, Bauer and Robbins use timeless Stoic wisdom to provide proven, award-winning strategies and great team-building activities that help education leaders find 'calm in the chaos.'"

Damon West, Bestselling Author of _The Coffee Bean_

"Political unrest, racial tensions, and unrealistic expectations are just some of the realities that educators face daily. In this book, Bauer and Robbins not only provide strategies for educational leaders to overcome these continuous waves of tension, but they also share thought-provoking team-building activities leaders can use to strengthen those around them."

Chris Singleton, Award-Winning Author and Keynote Speaker

"Written by two leaders who model how to lead with integrity, this book offers a refreshing perspective on leadership that is relevant in today's fast-paced profession. With insightful anecdotes and practical exercises, Glenn and Dan equip you with tools to navigate challenges with grace, maintain emotional balance, and reflect on how you can enjoy calmness in a leadership role while being your authentic self."

Marlon Styles, Education Speaker and Former Superintendent

"Glenn and Danny challenge school leaders to rethink, reevaluate, and remove the stress and chaos that are typical of our positions by embracing a Stoic framework that brings calm to the mind and soul. In doing so, they help us reimagine what leadership can and should be for each of us and those we lead."

Scott Rocco, Award-Winning Superintendent, Author, and Speaker

"This book is a compelling exploration of Stoic philosophy and how it applies to today's challenging school leadership landscape. Whether you're an educator taking your initial steps into leadership, eager to cultivate the skills and dispositions of an effective leader, or an experienced professional striving to maintain your edge amidst obstacles and challenges, this book serves as an essential guide for the development and application of wise leadership.

What sets the book apart is its genuine resonance; the stories woven throughout are authentic and relatable, evoking moments of recognition and introspection for every reader. Bauer and Robbins masterfully blend these real-world scenarios with deep-rooted Stoic principles, providing readers with thought-provoking ideas, hard-won knowledge, and opportunities to reflect on their professional practice.

Engaging, insightful, and truly beneficial, the book encourages readers to embrace the challenges and obstacles of their leadership roles and transform them into opportunities for growth and development. This book is more than just a great read—it is an experience that prompts thought, reflection, and action, empowering educators to lead with poise, balance, and a deep sense of purpose."

David Jakes, Educator and Author of *The Design Thinking Classroom*

"Glenn and Danny take ancient philosophy and apply it to modern leadership needs. Wisdom, justice, courage, and temperance take on new and relevant meaning through the reflective exercises, evidence from years of experience, and application to the needs of today's school leaders. In the pages of this great leadership book, you will find coaching, inspiration, and poetic simplicity of highly complex concepts. This will become a desk reference for every school leader everywhere."

Mike Lubelfeld, Public School Superintendent, Author, and Student of Leadership

"Are you trying to navigate difficult situations in your building or district? You are not alone. In this book, Bauer and Robbins share a wide variety of real-life examples of their own leadership challenges. More importantly, they give you a time-tested framework for understanding what is within your control and what is not. They show you that, no matter the situation, you can lead from a place of calm in the chaos."

Dr. Nick Polyak, Superintendent, Author, and Speaker

"Drawing upon the ancient wisdom of Stoicism and its timeless virtues, this book offers a compelling guide for today's educators navigating the tumultuous waters of school leadership. Through personal anecdotes and insightful scenarios, Bauer and Robbins illuminate the transformative power of wisdom, justice, courage, and temperance in confronting today's challenges.

As stress and uncertainty grip the realm of education, this work emerges as a beacon of hope, guiding leaders towards equanimity and steadfast purpose. An essential read for anyone in leadership, it brilliantly applies the lessons of the past to the complexities of the present to help educators create the dynamic experiences modern learners need for their future."

Thomas Murray, Bestselling Author of *Personal & Authentic* and Director of Innovation for Future Ready Schools Washington, D.C.

"This handy book provides educators with a state-of-the-art, evidence-based approach to better manage the multitude of stresses in their lives. It gives leaders a plethora of useful capabilities to apply to many aspects of life, including interpersonal challenges. Those who feel shackled to anxiety, high levels of stress, or mental health difficulties will find secrets to freeing themselves in this engaging and easy-to-read guide.

Any educator who takes seriously the social and interpersonal issues that their students encounter should read this book. You and the people you care about will benefit from its concise suggestions for building a better life. I highly recommend it!"

Devin C. Hughes, Speaker, Positive Psychology Researcher, and Author of *Simple Tips to Be a Happier YOU: Scientifically Proven to Help You Everyday*

"There is nothing more important than a leader who can bring forth a sense of calmness in the midst of chaos. But in many ways, chaos has become a guest that has decided to overstay its welcome, especially in our current context. Allow the stories on these pages from Daniel and Glenn to provide you with the thinking, support, and strategies to better deal with this unwanted guest that might not be leaving anytime soon."

David Culberhouse, Program Manager, Community Schools for the Southern Inland Regional Technical Assistance Center

"Our educators are providing students with knowledge, but are they providing them with wisdom? This book distills the core principles of the ancient philosophy of Stoicism into actionable steps that educators can use to become more effective leaders. While we provide our students with an education to prepare them for life, we also have an obligation to prepare them emotionally. *Calm in the Chaos* will help you be a more effective and Stoic educator. More importantly, it will help you develop Stoic students!"

Michael McGill, Author of *A Stoic a Day* and *Stoicism for IT Professionals*

CALM
IN THE
CHAOS

Ancient Stoic Wisdom for Successful School Leadership

Daniel Bauer & Glenn Robbins
with Ariel Curry

ISBN 979-8-9881350-4-3 (paperback) / ISBN 979-8-9881350-5-0 (ebook)

First publication: 2023

All personal stories and names throughout the book are used with permission from each respective individual.

CALM IN THE CHAOS

Ancient Stoic Wisdom for Successful School Leadership

INTRODUCTION

"If, at some point in your life, you should come across anything better than justice, honesty, self-control, courage . . . it must be an extraordinary thing indeed."

- Marcus Aurelius (2003, p. 30)

GLENN

I showed up to the school board meeting filled with a sense of dread. I knew it was going to be a tough night. Already a crowd was gathered to tear us apart.

I had tried to prepare the board members for what to expect. As the superintendent, I had been through this before, but for most of them, it was their first time being on the receiving end of the community's wrath.

And why were they angry?

It was an unfortunate situation; the district had lost some state funding, through no fault of our own, and we were forced to let some beloved staff go. Many in the community were furious.

The meeting went just about as bad as expected. It felt like we were lined up for the firing squad, and there could be no firing back. The people demanded an answer—but our hands were tied. Everything we did say was misconstrued and misinterpreted.

"Don't you have any empathy?" someone asked.

I breathed deeply and pictured a rock being pounded by the crashing waves. I felt my fellow school board members squirming in their discomfort, their temperatures rising under the onslaught. I would have to be the rock.

STILLNESS IN A WORLD OF CHAOS

The world around us is volatile; it changes constantly. Our schools are a microcosm of that chaos; they are touched by disorder, trauma, and turmoil on a daily basis. All of us have our stories—we've seen Machiavellian maneuverings amongst staff, kids suffering in poverty and abuse, unfair policies that hurt the most vulnerable, great intentions foiled by lack of funding or support, and a host of other problems.

Meanwhile, many of our colleagues are jumping ship—and who could blame them? A survey from NASSP (2022) reported that school leaders' stress levels are so high that over half of them are planning to leave the profession in the next three years.

No matter how noble your intentions, it's hard to continue when you feel constantly at the mercy of everything around you. Like a ship being battered by the waves, you wonder how you can ever recover your balance, let alone get where you're trying to go.

Most of us respond reactively. We can't help it. We're a product of the people we learn from, and most of us haven't had great mentoring. At best, we've figured out how to be leaders on our own. At worst, we've witnessed or been subject to political infighting and backstabbing that's made us cynical and wary of each other.

Many of us don't know how to trust our teams and delegate. Our own ego, reinforced by dozens of bad experiences, tells us that we are the only ones who can get a job done "right." And when we pile up responsibilities on ourselves, imposter syndrome takes over: *I'm a fraud; there's no way I can do all of this on my own.* And yet, our ego and fear of humiliation keep us stuck.

We all face challenges in our daily role as leaders in education. We want to meet those challenges with poise, confidence, groundedness, and flexibility. We want to take a stand for our students when we need to, respond to aggravations with kindness and forbearance whenever possible, recognize the good in the people around us, and know what the appropriate actions are for each circumstance. Most of all, we want to feel the sense of inner peace that comes with knowing we've done our best and the assurance that no matter what comes next, we have the inner tools needed to navigate these waters.

Thankfully, many leaders before us have faced the same challenges. Our goal in this book is to equip you with the mindset and timeless practices that have served leaders for centuries. We want to introduce you to an ancient philosophy that has provided leaders an incredible foundation of wisdom, temperance, courage, and justice—sustaining them with an unshakeable equanimity through every storm.

This ancient wisdom is found in Stoicism.

WHY STOICISM?

When most of us hear the word "stoic," we think of a person devoid of emotions, someone who represses their natural urges and builds a wall between themselves and the chaotic world. Actually, a Stoic is a person committed to the practice of *managing* and appropriately *regulating* their emotions, so that they might respond in the best way no matter what the situation calls for. This ancient school of philosophy was pursued in ancient Rome and developed over hundreds of years by a group of unlikely philosophers, including a shipwrecked merchant (Zeno), a crippled slave (Epictetus), and one of the greatest emperors who has ever lived (Marcus Aurelius).

More recently, Stoicism has seen a resurgence in popularity thanks to a college dropout who was inspired by a little book of *Meditations* by Aurelius: Ryan Holiday. Since Ryan published his first book on Stoicism, *The Obstacle Is the Way*, in 2014, millions of people have enjoyed discovering how this ancient philosophy applies to and benefits their daily lives. Including us.

DANNY ───────────────

It was my first year as a principal. I was new and ambitious. I loved the students and the staff. I had bold dreams for how to improve our school. I rode my skateboard around campus. I wanted to try new methods and challenge my staff to adopt new practices. Even then, I was a Ruckus Maker. But not everyone was as excited as I was.

Pretty soon, I started getting formally written up—nearly every week—by the area superintendent who had been vocal about her disagreement with my leadership. The write-ups were usually petty, seemingly insignificant. For example, I got written up for showing up at 7:02 a.m. instead of 7 a.m. I was written up for posting on social media during the work day, even though I had scheduled those posts while I was off the clock.

Later, I found out that my assistant principal was informing the area superintendent of any perceived infraction I committed. Eventually, their plan to force me out worked. I quit.

In the aftermath, I had to rethink my identity. I was heartbroken and angry. How could these others have stolen my dream? How could they be so narrow-minded, so unsupportive of a new leader? I fantasized about getting revenge.

And then I heard podcaster Tim Ferriss talking about this ancient philosophy called Stoicism. I read The Obstacle Is the Way *by Ryan Holiday. I realized that perhaps what I had viewed as a major setback in my life was actually an invitation to something better and even bolder than I had imagined.*

I started asking myself, "How can I turn this obstacle into an opportunity?"

I continued podcasting about how to support and build up new leaders. I started writing. I built a community of fellow Ruckus Makers who wanted the freedom to dream big and serve in new ways. I found a life and a calling that was even more fulfilling, with an even bigger impact, than I could have achieved if I had remained in the principalship.

Ultimately, I'm thankful for my experience because it pushed me to get creative and go all in on what I am supposed to do. Without that negative experience, I wouldn't have made my creative endeavors a full-time pursuit or had the time to mentor so many other leaders who needed support.

Stoicism has taught me to be grateful for every challenge and to see them as opportunities to grow.

GLENN

Growing up, my grandfather would constantly say, "It's not the problem that you have, it's how you handle it," whenever something would upset or anger me and others. To this day, I echo his words to my own children because he meant so much to me and our family. He was a WWII veteran, but he rarely spoke to me about his time serving as part of the world's Greatest Generation.

As I continued into college, I was a double major: history and education. During that time, I was eager to learn so much more about the war he fought in as well as where he might have picked up that saying. In my pursuit, I found Marcus Aurelius, Epictetus, Seneca, and many others that I still study to this very day.

While I'll never know where my grandfather learned it or whether he studied the ancients, I can't help but smile knowing how this timeless saying still resonates with much of what I do as a husband, father, and educator. Since that time, reading authors like Ryan Holiday and Robert Greene has continued my personal and professional journey into philosophy, which I've found especially helpful because school leadership calls for Stoicism daily.

We don't claim to be experts on Stoicism. Neither of us has a philosophy degree. Rather, having seen the power of Stoicism in our lives and in our leadership at schools—not just for us, but for the people we serve— we want to share it with you. There are many misunderstandings and critiques of Stoicism, so we're not going to try to convince you to adopt this way of thinking across the board (we'll leave that to Ryan Holiday and the Stoics themselves).

Instead, we simply want to focus on the four main virtues that Stoicism teaches and help you practice using them at school. The benefit will be greater emotional equanimity for you and the people you serve. Whether you're new to Stoic philosophy or have an entire bookshelf dedicated to it, you will be delighted to learn practices so useful you will see immediate results in your leadership.

ABOUT THIS BOOK

Cicero, one of the greatest documenters of Stoic philosophy—though not a Stoic himself, ironically—taught that the Stoics held four virtues above all:

> *"But whatever is right springs from one of four sources.*
> *It consists either in the perception and skilful treatment*
> *of the truth; or in maintaining good-fellowship with men,*
> *giving to every one his due, and keeping faith in contracts*
> *and promises; or in the greatness and strength of a lofty*
> *and unconquered mind; or in the order and measure that*
> *constitute moderation and temperance."*
> **▪ Cicero** (1887, Book I.5)

On the Daily Stoic (n.d.-a.), Ryan Holiday distills these descriptions into four words: **wisdom, justice, courage, and temperance**. The outcome of those four virtues is **equanimity**.

Wisdom: Cicero defines wisdom as "the investigation and discovery of truth." It is about the relentless pursuit of learning and education. We're all lifelong learners, right? But it's about more than just knowledge and facts; wisdom is knowing the difference between what we control and what we don't, between good and evil, between right and wrong—and then acting on that knowledge. Armed with wisdom, the other three virtues help us to live and operate with the people around us so that, as Cicero says, "the fellowship and union of society might be maintained."

Temperance: Like many other ancient wisdom traditions, Stoicism teaches to guard ourselves against extremes, to exhibit self-control in all situations. Temperance is the practice of order and moderation, of deliberating before acting, and of not being led by our impulses.

Courage: To be a "brave and great soul," as Cicero described, each of us needs courage to resist the comfort of the status quo and act with bravery and honor despite the cost. Courage helps us to turn down temptations, tackle challenges with eagerness and curiosity, and fight every day to be a person of character.

Justice: For the Stoics, justice was the foundation of all virtues and demonstrates our interconnectedness as a human race. When operating with justice, we injure no one and we take action to prevent the injuring of others. We prioritize the common good and exercise generosity as often as possible.

Equanimity: Once we have cultivated these four virtues in our lives, the end result is *ataraxia*, or equanimity—a calmness of mind and soul. When we temper our emotions with reason for the good of ourselves and those around us, we can enjoy a state of inner tranquility and peace. Isn't that what we all want?

This is the framework we will explore throughout the book. Each chapter will unpack one of the four Stoic virtues. You'll notice that all four of these virtues blend together. They rely on each other. Temperance may sometimes require wisdom, justice may require courage, and so on. In each chapter, we'll unpack the main ideas inherent in each virtue and offer three realistic (though hypothetical) school scenarios for you to practice these ideas.

We're convinced that upon finishing this book, you will know how to apply self-control and perseverance to help you manage your emotions, become an open-minded thinker, and grow to be an effective problem-solver. But don't just take our word for it.

We challenge you to think critically and test the ideas found in this book to see if they are worthy of your time and effort. Although we have thousands of years of examples and experience to prove these practices work, ultimately our opinion and experience does not matter. What matters most is that you validate these ideas and practices for yourself.

CHAPTER 1
WISDOM

knowledge · education · truth · self-reflection

"Wisdom is the oneness of mind that guides
and permeates all things."

· Heraclitus (2003, p. 10)

DANNY

One day, when I was a principal, a parent came in very upset. Her daughter had been in a fight with a boy—and she wanted the boy suspended. Thankfully, we could see the incident on our school camera footage. It revealed that her daughter had actually started the fight, attacking the boy from behind. The mother didn't care.

I tried my best to be empathetic, reflecting back to her: "This is what I heard you say . . . is this right?"

No matter how she felt, we had specific school policies and consequences that had to be enforced. I wrote out all of the policies and consequences on a white board. Patiently, I walked her through my options as the school leader and asked her to help me find the right consequence for her daughter (and for the boy, who fought back) within the limits I was working under. There was only so much in my control.

Thankfully, she recognized that truth and we were able to agree on consequences that felt fair to everyone.

REMEMBER WHAT YOU CONTROL AND WHAT YOU DON'T

"Happiness and freedom begin with a clear understanding of one principle: Some things are within our control, and some things are not."

▪ **Epictetus** (2013, p. 13)

Leadership often sounds like the key to greater freedom and autonomy. Surely when you get to make more decisions, you are more free!

But if you've been in leadership for a while, you know that's not true.

Often, leadership means *more* responsibility but *less* control over the situations you're meant to be leading.

The Stoics knew this as well. Epictetus, one of the most prolific Stoic philosophers, was born into slavery. His master was an advisor to the emperor Nero, so Epictetus could closely observe the lives of the most powerful men in the Roman Empire. But that didn't mean they were free.

Later, when Epictetus was legally freed, he thought deeply about the question of control and freedom and wrote extensively about how to handle situations in which we often have little or no control.

Often, school leaders waste a considerable amount of time worrying about (and trying to solve) things that are ultimately out of their control. But Epictetus would say: We have to play the cards we're dealt—and let everything else go.

So naturally, you might be thinking: *What is and is not in my control?*

What is in your control? Your actions.

What is out of your control? Everything else that does not fit inside the category of your actions.

For example, the following things are in your control:

- Your opinions
- Your goals
- How you choose to spend your time
- Your temper
- Your attitude
- Your character

And the following things are not in your control:

- Your students' lives
- The outcomes of your school's initiatives
- Your teachers' classrooms
- Your reputation (phew, that's a tough one!)
- The policies established by the school board and central office
- Parents and community members

The quickest path to being frustrated as a leader is misunderstanding what is in your control and trying to force certain outcomes from other people. Every leader who's tried to force staff to adopt a new technology, initiative, or protocol knows how difficult this is!

Similarly, what other people say about you (reputation) or the actions they decide to take at school are not in your control. And when those things are hurtful or disappointing, it can send you into a tailspin of negativity.

But if you can understand that other people and their actions are outside of your control, then you can choose not to be harmed. Stoics believed it wasn't the things outside our control that caused us distress and pain, but rather our view of those external events. Our opinions, which are within our control, are to blame.

You always have a choice about how you interpret others' actions—that is always within your control. You can choose to take them personally, or you can choose not to be harmed. Learning from Epictetus's writings, the emperor, Marcus Aurelius (2003), later wrote, "It doesn't hurt me unless I interpret its happening as harmful to me. I can choose not to" (p. 87).

In his book, *A Guide to the Good Life,* William Irvine adds one more nuance to the idea of control. According to Irvine (2008), "There are things over which we have complete control, things over which we have no control at all, and things over which we have some but not complete control" (p. 89).

We've already talked about the things we do and do not have complete control over. But what about that third category? Although not everything is in your control, many things are within your influence. In school, your leadership exists in this middle ground, a gray area where you can *influence* outcomes but not control them. What are examples of things you have *some* control over but not complete control?

Imagine you are a superintendent sitting on the school board. You cannot decide which members are voted in by the community, but you can certainly help to guide and educate those members on policies and procedures. You may not be able to stop certain books from being banned by the district, but you can advocate within the community. You cannot force students to study or learn, but you can give them all the tools they need for success.

Since you cannot control other people's actions or decisions, you would be wise to focus on becoming the best version of yourself.

PRACTICE WISDOM

After another successful school week, Principal Rosa awakens on a Saturday morning to the ping of notifications on her phone. Last night, while Principal Rosa was enjoying much-needed family time, a parent posted pictures of a book that her child was being "forced" to read, a book that she disagrees with. Friends of the parent were incensed and filled the school's contact form with angry messages. The social media post is going viral and commenters have even tagged local and national news outlets to try to bring attention to it. Now, on her day off, Principal Rosa finds herself fielding panicked texts from teachers, staff, and parents wondering what they should do.

REFLECT:

1. What is within Principal Rosa's control? What isn't?

2. Where might Principal Rosa exert influence?

3. If you were the school leader in this situation, what would you do?

COMMIT TO LEARNING

"Don't just say you have read books. Show that through them you have learned to think better, to be a more discriminating and reflective person. Books are the training weights of the mind."

• *Epictetus* (2013, p. 99)

So many of us might think of ourselves as "lifelong learners." It might even be in our profiles on social media! But can you think of a time when you rolled your eyes at a required PD day and dragged your feet to get there? How are you challenging yourself to learn more about the students within your community and their lived experiences? What education and leadership books have you not only read, but truly applied in your life and your school? When was the last time you tried learning a new skill and experienced the discomfort and cognitive dissonance of being a beginner—as your students do every single day?

Have you fallen into the trap of thinking, "I already know this"?

To attain wisdom, you must be willing to learn—and learning requires humility. Epictetus (1890) wrote, "What is the first business of one who studies philosophy? To part with self-conceit. For it is impossible for any one to begin to learn what he thinks that he already knows" (Book 2.17).

As a school leader, it is vital to be open-minded and willing to listen to different perspectives. Check your ego at the door, and listen empathetically to what people are saying.

Leaders are responsible for making decisions that affect the people they lead. If a leader is closed-minded and unable or unwilling to put themselves in the place of a learner, they may not be able to consider all of the options available to them, and they may make decisions that are not in the best interests of their people.

Your willingness and humility to learn is also one of the greatest examples you can set for your team and your students. If you aren't willing to engage in a PD day because you "already know this," why should your teachers? If you're "not an art person" and don't want to try learning how to create 3D models with the art class, why should your students try to wrap their heads around this complex skill?

PRACTICE WISDOM

Instructional Coach Carter has 10 classrooms to visit today, and he's running behind. He walks into Mrs. Cho's seventh grade biology class where they are learning about cell division and analyzing samples under a microscope. Planning to just stay a few minutes, Coach Carter starts checking items off of his checklist.

He can't help but notice one student who looks confused, glancing around at the other students to try to mimic what they're doing with the microscopes. Mrs. Cho is busy helping a group of girls as this student hides in the corner, painfully disengaged. Coach Carter considers trying to help but glances at his watch; just a few minutes before he needs to be in another classroom. Besides, when was the last time he used a microscope? Could he even remember how?

REFLECT:

1. What are Coach Carter's options for next steps?

2. What will happen to this student if he leaves now?

3. What would you do if you were Coach Carter?

OWN YOUR MISTAKES

"If anyone can refute me—show me I'm making a mistake or looking at things from the wrong perspective—I'll gladly change. It's the truth I'm after, and the truth never harmed anyone. What harms us is to persist in self-deceit and ignorance."

• **Marcus Aurelius** (2003, pp. 73-74)

As a "leader," as someone to whom others look for guidance and stability, it can be hard to admit when we are wrong. *What kind of leader am I if I make mistakes?* we might think. We fear losing trust and influence if the people we're leading know that we're fallible humans, just like everyone else.

All of us are far from perfect. We've all made countless mistakes along our professional journeys, and those mistakes are part of the journey. Many of us have taught the acronym FAIL (First Attempt In Learning) to our students and helped them see mistakes as learning opportunities. We graciously coach our colleagues and give them whatever support they need to improve. We comfort others when they mess up. The only ones we don't allow to make mistakes, though, are ourselves!

Here's the secret.

Your staff already knows you make mistakes. They probably see your mistakes more clearly than you do.

What if you welcomed that information? What if you modeled how you want other learners to view their mistakes? What if, instead of protecting your ego, you made it clear that you *want* others to tell you when you're missing something, when you messed up, or when you need to apologize so that you can correct it immediately?

When something goes wrong, be quick to point the finger at yourself before someone else. Own it!

According to author and speaker Danny Silk (2015), "being right doesn't have to be sacrificed, but having to be the one who is right needs to go" (Foreword, para. 4).

When you prove to others that you want to learn from your mistakes, the people around you will actually respect you more than you'll ever know. People love to follow authentic leaders who demonstrate that they, too, are human and working to be the best that they can. Shut your ego up, stop pointing fingers, own it, accept it, and work to correct it.

PRACTICE WISDOM

On a cheerful morning, Principal Daniels heads to Mrs. Meyer's room to conduct her spring evaluation. There were a few things they had discussed after her evaluation in the fall that he is hoping to see today. He slips into the back of the classroom as unobtrusively as possible, noting he has about 20 minutes to stay.

Everything seems to be going well—Mrs. Meyers is calm and engaging. She handles a small misbehavior graciously and keeps the rest of the class focused on their task. But he doesn't see one of the items they'd discussed last time, so he feels he can't check it off on the rubric.

At the end of his 20 minutes, he thanks Mrs. Meyers and heads out the door. He sends out her evaluation later that week with a good score but notes that the same issue has occurred again, and it needs to be corrected.

The next week, she calls him in tears.

"I did correct it!" she insists. "I did that the day before, but I didn't know which day you'd be visiting, so I just had to move forward with my teaching plan."

Principal Daniels's face flushes with embarrassment. Did he make a mistake? Could he trust that she is telling the truth?

REFLECT:

1. Have you ever been in a similar situation?

2. How might Principal Daniels address the discrepancy with this teacher? What should his next steps be?

3. Have you ever made a mistake and had it pointed out to you? How did you make it right (or not)?

FIND YOUR HEROS AND ANTIHEROS

"For we must indeed have someone according to whom we may regulate our characters; you can never straighten that which is crooked unless you use a ruler."

• **Seneca** (1917, p. 54)

For years, education has not evolved. The most common critique is that it is a "factory system" where the main focus has been to teach students compliance and prepare them for jobs that were common during the Industrial Revolution.

In this system, leaders are no more than managers—super-doers, legislators, and enforcers whose job is to make sure that everyone else stays in line. Unfortunately, that's still the most common model of leadership.

Excellent leadership role models are hard to find. Many school leaders *want* to be great leaders, to break out of the factory-system mold, but we haven't seen what good leadership looks like, so we stumble to put it into practice. Many of us have only seen examples of what *not* to do.

Try as we might, when we're surrounded by bad actors, they're likely to influence us. Jim Rohn's famous quote, "You're the average of the five people you spend the most time with" (Canfield & Switzer, 2005, p. 189), is usually the kick in the pants a leader needs to investigate the other leaders they spend the most time with and look to as mentors. Those people will give you the best hint at who *you* are as a leader.

You have to ask yourself: Are these people I want to be like?

In *Letters From a Stoic*, Seneca (1969) writes to his friend Lucillius about the importance of mentorship and encourages him to find someone whom Lucillius admires, someone he wouldn't want to disappoint. He writes about the tremendous gift it is to have an effective and encouraging mentor in your life, someone whom you can measure yourself against. The problem is, these mentors are few and far between.

But are they?

Maybe in the physical domain of your life.

If you find that you lack mentors, or the mentors you do have are not the ones you need, fear not. Countless biographies and autobiographies have been written by some of the greatest leaders history has ever known. Browse the shelves of your school library; you'll find plenty.

Then there are all the classic Stoic texts that we cite throughout this book. Aurelius wrote *Meditations* while serving as the ruler of one of the largest empires that has ever existed. During his reign, he faced many leadership obstacles: attempted coups, political infighting, annoying coworkers, and even a pandemic. Sound familiar?

History is filled with great leadership heroes who have managed situations *exactly* like the one you're going through. This is why the Stoics saw reading as one of the best ways to develop wisdom—because through books, you can learn from the greatest minds that have ever lived.

And what about the antiheroes, the people you want to be nothing like?

You can be thankful for them, too. Yes, avoid behaving like them and surround yourself with better mentors—but do watch the antiheroes. Watch how they act and how their actions impact the people around them. Watch how they continue to keep education stuck. Learn from their mistakes.

Then ask yourself: What kind of leader do I want to be?

PRACTICE WISDOM

Superintendent Beckett has just been hired to her first superintendency, and she is stoked. Throughout the weeks of the interview process and getting to know various people within the school system, she's gathered a list of over 30 changes and long-term goals she wants to start implementing right away. This district has a lot of problems, but Superintendent Beckett has a vision for how to improve things.

Her predecessor in the district was considered a bit of a lame duck—no vision, just someone checking things off the list. Not so for her! She has energy and enthusiasm and is excited to get started. This district hired her to get things done, and she is determined to start things off with a bang.

When Superintendent Beckett meets with her new executive assistant, though, she is cautioned to be careful, to go slow and get to know everyone first before making a lot of changes. Superintendent Beckett is frustrated by their conversation. Is her new EA trying to hold her back? Will she face opposition from others? Is this the start of an agonizing relationship?

REFLECT:

1. Have you ever been in a situation like this? What did you do?

2. If you were a mentor in Superintendent Beckett's life, how would you advise her?

3. How could Superintendent Beckett get the relationship with her EA off on the right foot?

CHAPTER 2
JUSTICE

fairness · service · fellowship · goodness
kindness · integrity

"Therefore I would have brave and high-spirited
men, also good and simple, friends of truth,
remote from guile—traits of character which
belong to the very heart of justice."

· *Cicero* (1887, Book 1.19)

DANNY

There were two STEM educators in my building. They were both effective and well liked by their kids for different reasons. There was just one problem. They hated each other!

Neither of the teachers mentioned their feud to me; the only way I found out was through our instructional coach who was trying to help them sort out their differences. I encouraged her to try to resolve it with them before I got involved.

Unfortunately, after a few weeks, their hatred of each other was only getting worse. It was hurting the department culture, and the instructional coach was at her wit's end trying to get these two to work together. I had to step in.

I scheduled observations and individual meetings with both teachers and asked them how things were going. Both of them reported, "No problems here! Everything's fine!," which was obviously a lie.

So I went back to them both and told them what the instructional coach had reported to me. "You haven't been honest with me," I said. "I've heard multiple times from one of our coaches, who has no reason to lie to me, that you're being terrible to each other and acting immaturely."

Then I laid out my plan for them:

"Tomorrow morning, the three of us are meeting at Starbucks to work this out. I've already got your classes covered and we're not docking your pay—but you can't come back to this building tomorrow until we get this resolved. And you're going to tell me the truth. Now, what's your favorite coffee? Drinks are on me."

The next morning, when I arrived at Starbucks, the two teachers were already there. They already had their drinks—and one for me, too—and they'd already hashed it out. I listened to them explain everything, and we agreed on a plan for how they were going to work together going forward.

After that, they never had any problems working together. I was proud that they stepped up and finally resolved things themselves. And I was proud of myself for giving them the opportunity to step up and do the right thing.

STAY HUMBLE

"To escape imperialization—that indelible stain. It happens. Make sure you remain straightforward, upright, reverent, serious, unadorned, an ally of justice, pious, kind, affectionate, and doing your duty with a will. Fight to be the person philosophy tried to make you."
- Marcus Aurelius (2003, p. 75)

Think back to all of the times when you were in the interview chair, hopeful that someone would believe in you enough to give you a shot as a teacher's aide, teacher, coach, supervisor, assistant principal, principal, athletic director, central office administrator, and/or superintendent. You believed in the best for your students and staff, and you wanted to make a positive change in the world for the better. You felt you had to work hard to prove that you were there for the right reasons.

Then it happened—you got the job.

When you've been recognized for your efforts, it's easy to start to believe that you *deserve* to be there, that you really must know what's best. Your ego starts to sneak up on you from time to time, and when that happens, you forget your true purpose: to serve the people around you.

This is why justice starts with humility: Because to serve others, to advocate for the common good, you must be able to put aside your own ego.

Marcus Aurelius was crowned *Imperator Caesar*, meaning that he was the military leader and ruler of the Roman Empire. Later, the title *Augustus*, which signified a divine appointment, was added. He was in every way— spiritually, militarily, and organizationally—the leader of the largest empire on earth at the time. It would have been easy for him to think that he was always right, to always insist on his way as many other emperors before and after him did.

Yet, in his journals, Aurelius reminded himself not to let those titles go to his head. He reminded himself constantly that his job, the job he was privileged to have, was to use the short time he was given to fight for the common good.

You must not let your accolades go to your head. The only thing that a trophy or a piece of paper in a frame will do is collect dust. You're here to serve, not collect fancy titles or trophies. You must always remain humble.

Quick test: When you introduce yourself to someone else in your school/ district, is it, "I'm Dr. [insert last name here], and I am the [position] at this district," or is it, "Hi, my name is [insert first name here]." Last time we checked, we are all human beings. Do you really need to remind everyone else of your titles? If you need to announce yourself as a leader, are you really a leader?

PRACTICE JUSTICE

Curriculum Director Williams is attending a national conference looking for a new math curriculum. He arrives a few minutes early and browses the vendor hall, looking at all of the exciting edtech products available. At one of the vendor booths, a tall young man tells him all about their incredible product. Williams is intrigued; this product would be a huge help to the math department, and the salesman is offering a bulk discount.

Williams is really flattered; the salesman seems like a kind, authentic young man. He's a former teacher, like himself, and the salesman really seems to get what their struggles are. Williams feels drawn in; he could be friends with this guy. He has the authority to make the call but hesitates, wondering if he should run it past a few of the teachers first to get their buy-in.

The salesman can sense that Williams is waffling. He turns up the charm, asking more thoughtful questions and flattering him.

"Hey, you know what?" the salesman says. "You're doing great work out there. How about I throw in something for you, too?" He pulls a few $100 gift cards from his pocket and tucks them in Williams's suit pocket with a grin.

Williams is shocked. Is this a bribe?

REFLECT:

1. How common is this type of behavior in your environment?

2. How can you protect your ego from flattery and avoid unethical behavior?

3. What helps you to stay humble in your position?

BE KIND

"For man, evil consists in injustice and cruelty and indifference to a neighbor's trouble, while virtue is brotherly love and goodness and justice and beneficence and concern for the welfare of one's neighbor."

• **Musonius Rufus** (2015, Lecture XIV:9)

Just be nice—it's that simple.

As the leader, we often have the power to approve or deny. We have the power to be gracious or strict. Most of us want to assume the best in others. We want to give latitude as often as we can. Yet it's also natural to worry that if we're too gracious, people might begin to take advantage of us.

Have you ever wondered if all the doctors in your community only have appointments available around school arrival or dismissal times? You've probably received an email or call to your office asking, "Can I leave 20 minutes early (or arrive 20 minutes late) because I have a doctor's appointment?" If you haven't received that email yet, buckle up. It's coming your way soon.

When you're dealing with everyone's requests, everyone's needs, it can be easy to think they're all ganging up on you.

The truth is, you have no idea what people are dealing with in their lives. Being a leader in a school requires you to be a jack-of-all-trades, yet taking care of your staff needs to be at the top of the list. Sickness, cancer, death of a loved one, divorce, depression. Everyone is dealing with something.

The questions you need to be asking are: Are my people OK? Can I give the person in front of me the benefit of the doubt? How can I see the person in front of me as an individual with their own unique needs and circumstances instead of just one more person in a line asking for something?

Too often, you let your emotions get the best of you and focus only on the negatives of the request that requires extra work on your part.

Instead, take a minute to thank them for making their day more chaotic for the better of the school/district, fellow staff who would have to cover them since there are no subs, and most importantly, the students. Take a minute to show that you care, and see how you can serve them.

When you are the first to serve, you set the example for everyone else. Compassion fuels justice.

PRACTICE JUSTICE

It's Friday, and Assistant Principal Henderson has been looking forward to this afternoon all week. She's excited to join in on the 100th-day-of-school assembly and participate in some friendly competition with the staff and students. At 12:50 p.m., 10 minutes before the assembly begins and right as she is about to walk down to the gym, a teacher and student show up at her door.

"Could we chat with you, Mrs. Henderson?" the teacher asks.

She can see the student has been crying and wonders what's going on. Probably bad behavior. Does this conversation really need to happen now? Don't they know the assembly is about to start? Couldn't it wait?

REFLECT:

1. If you were in AP Henderson's shoes, what questions would you ask?

2. How could AP Henderson make this student and teacher feel welcomed and prioritized despite the inconvenience to her schedule?

3. How do you work to make every individual in front of you feel like they belong?

PROTECT OTHERS

"Of injustice there are two kinds—one, that of those who inflict injury; the other, that of those who do not, if they can, repel injury from those on whom it is inflicted."

• Cicero (1887, Book I.7)

It's not enough to simply do good for others, to avoid inflicting injury, and hope for the best. If you do not protect others from injury as well, you're part of the problem.

You're probably thinking, "Of course I protect others from injury! I would never stand by!"

But ask yourself this: Do I *know* of all of the injuries that might be happening in my school under my watch? Who are the most vulnerable people in my school? What would *they* say about their school experience? Does everyone truly feel welcomed as part of the community?

In his book, *No Name in the Street*, writer and civil rights leader James Baldwin wrote:

> If one really wishes to know how justice is administered in a country, one does not question the policemen, the lawyers, the judges, or the protected members of the middle class. One goes to the unprotected—those, precisely, who need the law's protection most!—and listens to their testimony (p. 149).

The most vulnerable in your school and district are the ones who need your protection most. Do whatever you can to seek them out and know them. Make it your personal mission to advocate for their needs.

PRACTICE JUSTICE

Mr. Hughes has been a teacher at his school for 15 years. By now, he knows pretty much everyone in the school—or thinks he does. One day, he notices two of his students having a dispute during class. One is Evan. Mr. Hughes knows Evan well; he taught Evan's brother and sister, and Evan's mom is a regular volunteer at the school. Evan is gregarious and loud but generally a good kid.

"Mr. Hughes, David started it!" Evan whines. Mr. Hughes looks at David. He realizes he doesn't know much about David except that his parents are immigrants from Mexico—or maybe Honduras? He can't remember; he's never met them. David doesn't speak much in class and usually keeps to himself. Mr. Hughes knows he needs to resolve this issue quickly before the rest of the class starts to get bored and lose focus.

REFLECT:

1. What questions should Mr. Hughes ask?

2. How can Mr. Hughes foster a better relationship with David and all of his students?

3. What blind spots might need addressing? As Mr. Hughes's leader, how would you help him address those blind spots?

RESIST VENGEANCE

"Leave other people's mistakes where they lie."

• Marcus Aurelius (2003, p. 122)

When you think of a character in a movie looking for "justice," what is it that they're actually looking for? Vengeance. Our understanding of justice has, in many ways, been degraded to the idea of tit for tat, of score-keeping, of repaying one another's bad deeds with more bad deeds.

The Stoics challenge us to raise the bar.

As we just discussed, we all have an obligation to advocate for and take action on behalf of the marginalized, injured, and oppressed. We have an obligation to restore dignity. You might even argue that we have an obligation to allow others to feel the consequences of their actions when they do something wrong. These consequences actually further the common good.

But to perpetrate further harm by exacting revenge? That's where the Stoics draw the line. "To do harm is to do yourself harm. To do an injustice is to do yourself an injustice—it degrades you," said Aurelius (2003, p. 119).

Still, it's quite difficult to resist getting back at someone. What's the worst name/thing you were ever called or accused of growing up? You probably felt angry, hurt, and totally justified in name-calling right back, even if you were able to stop yourself from doing so.

But that experience is probably small potatoes compared to what you've experienced as a school leader. This role isn't for the weak of heart. All leaders, including school administrators, have been and always will be easy for the public to criticize.

Leadership can be compared to being in a fish bowl in the middle of a shooting range. Regardless of where you try to turn, everyone can see you, and everyone can fire remarks at you. There will be crude comments, hate, threats, slandering your name on any platform that will listen, and petitions asking for your removal because you made a decision that wasn't to someone else's liking. As shared in the Introduction, other school leaders may even conspire against you.

The world is full of Machiavellian people who work *against* the common good. Your duty is, as Aurelius said, to leave their bad deeds where they are and focus on preserving your own good character.

Follow the law, school policies, mission, and vision of where you work. Work together with your team to make informed decisions. Constantly communicate with your school board members, as there should never be any surprises. Always "read the room" before speaking to the room. Remember what you said in your interview chair before you were hired and who you serve each day. Be strong and kind, as what you do in response to others' bad behavior will not be long forgotten. Your dignity and character should always prevail.

PRACTICE JUSTICE

Ms. Foster has been making Principal Parker's life miserable all year long. She was a runner-up for his position, and unfortunately (for her), she didn't get the job. Since then, she's been a thorn in his side—bad-mouthing him to parents, contradicting him in front of the staff at meetings, and once, even taking credit for one of his ideas in front of the superintendent. To say Parker is angry would be an understatement.

And now it's evaluation time. Principal Parker heads to Ms. Foster's room, ready to look for any possible infraction or mistake. Wouldn't it be great to see her face when he gives her a bad review?

He sits for 20 minutes, the usual amount of time, watching eagle-eyed for anything he can mark her down on. There's nothing. He stays another 10 minutes, and then all the way till the end of the class. Finally, he has to admit she's a pretty good teacher.

But that doesn't mean he has to give her a good review. She certainly wouldn't do the same for him. He sits in his office and contemplates his options.

REFLECT:

1. Have you ever felt like Principal Parker?

2. Have you ever been tempted, or given into the temptation, to exact revenge when something didn't go your way?

3. How do you remain focused on the job in front of you and ensure that you do the right thing?

CHAPTER 3
COURAGE

bravery · fortitude · honor · sacrifice

"Give me courage to meet hardships; make me calm in the face of the unavoidable."

▪ **Seneca** (1917, p. 218)

GLENN

I started a new superintendent position on an island in New Jersey in February 2020—just one month before COVID-19 broke out and everything shut down. I had no idea what we were really dealing with and what was going to happen. I was supposed to go to a national conference in March, but instead, I stayed home to try to figure out the situation.

I sat down with our security officer to try to make a plan for school safety, but we quickly realized that this was unlike anything we'd ever dealt with before. I was worried about so many of the kids in our community and what would happen to them while school was shut down. I worried about foreclosures, domestic violence, drug and alcohol abuse, food scarcity, and more.

At the time, I was reading Stanley A. McChrystal's book Team of Teams. We decided to gather our own "team of teams" with people in the community and the district to create a plan together. We brought in the city manager, office of emergency management, public works, food services, teacher leaders, and even the chiefs of police and fire. Anybody and everybody who was a leader on the island was in that meeting.

I didn't know anyone from the community in that room; I'd only barely met my own staff. I had no idea how they'd react. I was worried that everyone would have their own priorities, that no one would be on the same page while talking to each other.

Mustering my courage, I told them we needed to figure out a plan together. We spent hours hashing out all of the details: How were we going to make sure kids had food? How were they going to arrive on the bus? How were we going to reach the homeless kids? How would we handle IEPs? What's the process for cleaning the facilities and getting more cleaning supplies and PPE? We delegated, and everyone took responsibility for their part. By the end of that meeting, we had a game plan.

Over the next several months, we continued hosting the team-of-teams meeting on Zoom, brought in other leaders, checked on the mental health of everyone, and asked for insight from every group in the community to build a plan for all scholars and staff to return with a regular full-day schedule. (Much of the country was creating modified schedules.) It wasn't easy with so much uncertainty in the world at the time, but when you work with an amazing group of leaders focused together as one, anything is possible.

As we prepared to return from lockdown several months later, we held a Zoom meeting with all of the parents and community members to share the plan with them. Our plan was so thorough, there were zero questions from the entire community after that meeting.

In the following weeks, that team of teams stayed in constant communication, making updates to the plan as we learned new information. Everyone continued to stay engaged and active in protecting our scholars and staff. In October of 2020, we were able to reopen the school seamlessly.

The beauty of it all is that we were recognized as the Safety and Security District of the Year by the Joint Insurance Funds and selected as a Digital Promise League of Innovative Schools. To be awarded these honors during chaotic times was a testament to everyone working together as one team for the greater good of others.

RELINQUISH FEAR

"There are more things, Lucilius, likely to frighten us than there are to crush us; we suffer more often in imagination than in reality."

• **Seneca** (1917, p. 67)

When we are in the thick of things, when the stakes and emotions are high, it's easy to believe that whatever we are facing could last forever.

Years ago when I (Danny) lived in Scotland, I had a horrible toothache. This was a big deal for me because I had never had so much as a cavity before.

When I went to the dentist, who must have been a novice, she told me to take some paracetamol and see her in a few weeks if it didn't get any better. She did no X-rays on my mouth, and I didn't think to ask.

The next day, I boarded a flight to Cyprus to visit some friends and spend time in the mountains. The pain got worse and worse. My face began to swell. The throbbing was so intense, I cried and could barely sleep.

Lying awake at night in Cyprus as my jaw throbbed, I thought, "Will this last forever?" For a moment, I even thought, "This is the end."

When I returned home, I immediately saw a new dentist who did the proper X-rays. My tooth was infected; I would need a root canal. He did some quick work that relieved the pain almost immediately. And in a few months I was back to normal.

I count myself fortunate that I was born in a time with access to modern medicine. If I had been born 200, 500, or 1,000 years earlier, the infection might have indeed killed me—a middle aged man.

It might seem crazy to you that I was so afraid of my toothache (although if you had felt it yourself, you would understand!). But that's how fear works; it grows in our minds like a weed, nearly impossible to uproot.

Other experiences in my life have also caused fear to take hold: a fight with my wife, the death of my father, and so on. Just like the toothache, these experiences often feel like they will last forever, but they do not.

The only permanent thing about experience is impermanence.

As school leaders, there are some experiences we just cannot escape from. They might be as small as a disciplinary meeting with unhappy parents or as large as a global pandemic. Either way, our position calls for us to step up and face whatever it is we fear. Our fears, both the real ones and the mountains we create in our imaginations, are useless. Fear does not make the situation go away; it only delays our facing it.

Seneca wrote often about fear in his letters to his friend, Lucilius. Seneca was no stranger to fear: He lived in the shadow of a mysterious disease and was banished multiple times by capricious emperors. Eventually, he was commanded to commit suicide.

Fear is a common theme in his writing—as is anger, which we'll discuss more in Chapter 4. Nevertheless, Seneca was clear on his priorities, and he knew that the solution was not to escape from his trials but to become the kind of person who could face them with courage: "If you really want to escape the things that harass you," he wrote, "what you're needing is not to be in a different place but to be a different person" (Daily Stoic, n.d.-b., "Quotes" section).

PRACTICE COURAGE

Dr. Greene gets a call during fourth period and learns that a large group of students across grade levels are walking out of their classes in silent protest of the school dress code.

"They're in the courtyard," the teacher on the phone tells her. "They all deserve detentions for walking out like that!"

Dr. Greene asks a couple of the student leaders to meet with her to explain their thoughts. The students tell her how the dress code discriminates against students of color. She can see immediately that they're right, but she hesitates. There are several teachers on staff who have been vocal about the dress code, often citing violations and sending kids who "refuse to cooperate" to Dr. Greene's office.

Honestly, it's no surprise that things have come to a head. Dr.

Greene is on the students' side, but she's afraid that if she tries to change the dress code, she'll face significant backlash from many of her teachers.

REFLECT:

1. Have you ever been in a situation where you knew that doing the right thing would be met with backlash?

2. How can Dr. Greene advocate for her students and set the right expectations for teachers through this scenario?

3. What strategies do you have for confronting your fears?

EMBRACE CHALLENGES

"The only contestant who can confidently enter the lists is the man who has seen his own blood, who has felt his teeth rattle beneath his opponent's fist, who has been tripped and felt the full force of his adversary's charge, who has been downed in body but not in spirit, one who, as often as he falls, rises again with greater defiance than ever."

• Seneca (1917, p. 66)

The Stoics often remind us that challenges are a necessary part of the journey to success. Remember what we learned in Chapter 1 on wisdom: We have to know the difference between what we control and what we don't.

Unfortunately, most of what lands in the category of what we don't control are obstacles we never invited into our lives and certainly don't want to face—especially when we have so many goals that we're trying to accomplish for the sake of our students, our staff, and our schools.

But it'll be easier if we expect that challenges will come, and we embrace them with as much dignity and patience as we can muster.

We can also turn those challenges into opportunities to become better. Whether it's that teacher we just can't seem to make happy or the parents who are constantly frustrated about our policies, we cannot grow if we don't allow friction in our lives, if we run away from conflict or try to avoid making people angry. It's not possible anyway, so we might as well embrace it and use it to our benefit. Doing so repeatedly over time will build our confidence.

That confidence proves useful when facing the criticism that inevitably comes with being in a position of authority. In a speech perhaps inspired by Seneca's words, President Theodore Roosevelt reminds us that we can't allow those critics to stop us from fighting:

> It is not the critic who counts: not the man who points out how the strong man stumbles or where the doer of deeds could have done better. The credit belongs to the man who is actually in the arena, whose face is marred by dust and sweat and blood, who strives valiantly, who errs and comes up short again and again, because there is no effort without error or shortcoming, but who knows the great enthusiasms, the great devotions, who spends himself in a worthy cause; who, at the best, knows, in the end, the triumph of high achievement, and who, at the worst, if he fails, at least he fails while daring greatly, so that his place shall never be with those cold and timid souls who knew neither victory nor defeat (Theodore Roosevelt Center, n.d.).

This is the spirit of strength and courage that the Stoics advocate for: a relentless refusal to be cowed, intimidated, or turned away from the pursuit of what's right.

PRACTICE COURAGE

Helen is the principal at an urban elementary school. She wakes up feeling great one morning and decides to arrive at the office 30 minutes earlier than normal, bringing with her coffee and breakfast for the staff. However, when Helen pulls into the parking lot, there is a couple waiting by the front door. Upon walking to the door with the coffee and breakfast, Helen can see the mother is red in the face.

"I hope you read the email that I sent last night," the mother declares icily. Helen continues to walk slowly towards the couple, asks for their names, and wonders if she should even open the door to let them in. So much for thinking that this is going to be a great morning.

The couple responds with their names. Helen has heard of this family before, and what she's heard was never good. These parents have a reputation for bulldozing their way over staff and manipulating leaders to get whatever they want. They love to mention their well-known lawyer if anyone dares to disagree with them.

Feeling that it is the right thing to do, Helen opens the doors and invites them in. She places the coffee and breakfast on one side of the conference table of the main office and then asks the couple to sit with her.

Helen asks when the email was sent; the last time she had checked her email was at 8 p.m. the night before. She had set a policy with staff and community leaders that if anything was urgent at night that couldn't wait until morning, they were to call her directly.

The mother had sent the email at 1:25 a.m. When Helen explains her policy, the mother responds with a number of words that you wouldn't use in a PG-rated movie. The father joins in the tirade, and it doesn't take too long before their lawyer's name is mentioned.

Helen takes a deep breath and considers how to respond.

REFLECT:

1. What other information is Helen missing?

2. Have you ever felt backed into a corner in your role? How did that situation resolve?

3. How could Helen plan ahead to set boundaries and build a more positive relationship with these parents?

EXPECT THE UNEXPECTED

"In this way you must understand how laughable it is to say, 'Tell me what to do!' What advice could I possibly give? No, a far better request is, 'Train my mind to adapt to any circumstance.'"

· Epictetus (Daily Stoic, n.d.-c., Section 1)

To be a school leader in today's world requires that you understand and embrace VUCA leadership: volatility, uncertainty, complexity, and ambiguity. The greatest school leaders admit that they do not have all the answers, but they help their school/district teams accept the realities of a VUCA world.

Leading a school in a VUCA world isn't about adopting the newest technologies that promise quick solutions, though. It's about finding the tools the school needs to be able to continue doing (and improving) its work within an ever-changing technological environment. The COVID-19 pandemic was, in many ways, a much-needed wake-up call for many districts who struggled to continue serving their students when they couldn't be together in person.

It's easy to get comfortable with what you know; it's much harder to maintain the attitude of a constant learner and humble yourself to be open to new ideas. It's difficult to imagine a world very different from the one you've always known. Yet the Stoics teach us: Expect the unexpected. And to the best of your ability, help your team to do the same.

Many school districts have a position you might not have heard of, but you've definitely noticed it. It's called the Chief "Yeah, But" Officer (CYBO). This person's comments go something like this:

"Yeah, but I've done it this way for 30 years, and it's never been a problem before."

"Yeah, but what if [insert idea they don't like] fails?"

"Yeah, but that would never work in my classroom/school/district."

As a leader, how have you prepared and trained your team and/or staff to embrace VUCA? Are they given the freedom to fail without the fear of becoming a failure? Do they have the psychological safety to know that you will support them when they present ideas that push the boundaries of traditional schooling? Can your team of diverse perspectives disagree with you and/or others in meetings without the fear of retaliation? Do you embrace the ideas of your innovators, or do you follow the beliefs of the CYBO in the district?

If you continuously follow the traditional scripts of outdated best practices—because that's how you learned best, that's what you learned from your mentor, or because of the CYBO—then how do you expect others to change their minds and adapt to any circumstance? Be the school leader you needed when you were a teacher instead of the one you resented.

PRACTICE COURAGE

For the past several weeks, the rumor mill in the community has been spiraling faster than a tornado. Everywhere Superintendent Muñoz looks, people are asking if everything is going to be OK. On the news, in social media feeds, at the school sporting events, around town—just about anywhere people congregate—the heated topic is there.

Earlier in the month, the state government body required a controversial curriculum revision be made to all public school districts in the state for the upcoming year. The latest rumor is that people are going to be lined up for hours wanting to speak during the public portion of the next school board meeting and city/town council meeting. Superintendent Muñoz is already starting to stress out and dread going to the meeting.

REFLECT:

1. What options does Superintendent Muñoz have? What are the different ways she might handle this situation?

2. How can she avoid becoming the CYBO?

3. How do you prepare teachers and staff for the realities of a VUCA world while honoring their autonomy and preferences?

FIGHT TO BE BETTER

"No matter what anyone says or does, my task is to be good. Like gold or emerald or purple repeating to itself, 'No matter what anyone says or does, my task is to be an emerald, my color undiminished.'"

- **Marcus Aurelius** (2003, p. 87)

We all face temptations from time to time. Temptations to take the path of least resistance or to choose what's best for you over what's best for your school. Temptations to give up when faced with poverty and trauma and bureaucracy and bickering and sadness.

It takes courage to stay devoted to your *why*.

It takes courage to stay devoted to your vision, your hope for a better future.

It takes courage to remember who you truly are and not to let the negative circumstances or obstacles that you face obscure the brilliance of your true colors.

Sometimes, we can fool ourselves into believing that we are courageous because we dare to rebel or make a scene. We believe in being Ruckus Makers in education—but not because we love chaos or anarchy. We believe in being Ruckus Makers for a purpose: to make schools and the people within them better. What matters here is motivation: Are we doing it on behalf of our students and the common good? Or are we doing it to serve ourselves?

Daring for your own benefit may be brave—but it's not courageous. The Stoics are firm on this point. Courage is the willingness to face danger for the sake of the common good.

PRACTICE COURAGE

Mr. Ramirez is a new instructional coach at one of the best schools in the state. He's lucky to have been hired there—all of his new colleagues have congratulated him, and his old colleagues are envious. He's also part of the leadership team. At one of their first meetings, the principal shares the school's most recent test results with pride, noting their overall high performance.

The meeting moves on to other agenda items, but Mr. Ramirez glances through the report more closely. He notices that although overall scores are high, when looking at the breakdown of students, he can see that many of those from low socioeconomic backgrounds are still struggling. They haven't been making the same gains—and even worse, when he digs further into their history, he can see that this problem has been occurring for the last few years. He brings it up to another teacher, but she shrugs it off.

"Look, we're a blue ribbon school. What more do you want? We can't make everyone happy."

Mr. Ramirez is shocked. Is this the attitude here? He wonders if he should avoid the topic at the next leadership team meeting. After all, he's still the new guy.

REFLECT:

1. What should Mr. Ramirez's next steps be?

2. What might the consequences be if he brings this problem up to the leadership team?

3. How can you prepare to do the right thing, regardless of the consequences?

CHAPTER 4
TEMPERANCE

self-control · discretion · moderation
composure · balance

"If you do the job in a principled way, with diligence, energy and patience, if you keep yourself free of distractions, and keep the spirit inside you undamaged, as if you might have to give it back at any moment . . . then your life will be happy. No one can prevent that."

· *Marcus Aurelius* (2003, p. 33)

DANNY

When I was being certified to be an administrator, my principal gave me some administrative responsibilities. So that I could complete those tasks, I was given a master key to the school, which included access to all of the rooms in the English building.

The chair of the English department—who was also our union president—often didn't show up to school. She was there, on average, just three days a week. And because of the way the school was set up, her room had the only access to the English department's book room. Whenever she wasn't there, the other teachers couldn't access the book room to get materials for their lessons. It was a perpetual problem, and everyone was annoyed.

I decided the right thing to do was open the room for the other teachers on the days when she wasn't there. Pretty soon, she heard what I was doing and demanded to meet with me.

I'd heard of a book called Crucial Conversations, *so I read it twice, took notes, and practiced the scripts in preparation for this meeting. Then, I offered to have the meeting in her room, on her turf, so that she would feel more comfortable. I felt as ready as I could be.*

The one thing I forgot to do was give her her script!

As much as I had prepared, I didn't anticipate her reaction. She accused me of stealing union documents to give to the administration—an idea that had never even occurred to me since I was part of the union! I got so frustrated with her ridiculous accusations that I couldn't hear or respond appropriately to the fears and concerns she had expressed.

When she demanded that I give the key back to our principal, I leaned over the table and held the key two inches from her nose.

"I'll give this back over my dead body!"

With that, I stormed out of the room.

That afternoon, I realized that I had seriously harmed the relationship, and I apologized. That was me clearly not being very Stoic.

LISTEN FIRST

"The reason why we have two ears and only one mouth is that we may listen the more and talk the less."

• Zeno, as quoted by Diogenes Laertius (1925, Chapter 1.23)

If we're being honest, most of us love talking more than listening. After all, we're all teachers at heart—and a big part of teaching is talking.

Unfortunately, all of the practice we get talking and giving directions doesn't necessarily prepare us to lead in the more subtle and diplomatic ways we need to when in positions of authority.

We have to learn to listen.

Remember, leadership is about service.

Listen with the intent to hear instead of listening to respond, and you'll be more likely to learn what is truly bothering a student. Listen to your staff when they tell you about the valid needs they have. Listen to the parents who express their fears and concerns for their childrens' education and welfare. The students, teachers, staff, and community you serve want and need to be heard.

All of us share this universal human need to know that we matter. After decades of interviewing guests on *The Oprah Winfrey Show*, Oprah shared that after the interviews were conducted and the cameras were turned off, every single guest wanted the same thing: to be validated.

> If I could reach through this television and sit on your sofa or sit on a stool in your kitchen right now, I would tell you that every single person you will ever meet shares that common desire. They want to know: "Do you see me? Do you hear me? Does what I say mean anything to you?" (Winfrey, 2011, p. 7).

By listening, by holding back your tongue and prioritizing the needs of the person in front of you, you will show that you care.

PRACTICE TEMPERANCE

Superintendent Rogers is exhausted. He's just gotten through another budgeting cycle and has been putting out fires for the past six months. One day, one of the principals—always a squeaky wheel, to be honest—calls with another complaint about drugs found on campus. He is asking for more school officers to be hired to help him regulate this problem. Just last month, the same principal had called and asked for another school counselor, which Rogers fought tooth and nail to get for him.

Rogers knows the resources are needed, but they just made it through a tough round of budget cuts, and he knows the money's not there. He's tempted to cut the man off and hang up the phone. Why bother listening if he can't do anything about it?

ACT WITH DISCRETION

"In good fortune or adversity, it is the good will with which you perform deeds that matters—not the outcome."

· Epictetus (2013, p. 103)

Just because rumors, gossip, and drama abound doesn't mean you have to stop and address each and every situation. As a school leader, you will be bombarded with requests and petitions and complaints, yet you have to distinguish what's worth hearing.

If this sounds like a contradiction to the last section—to listen more, to show that you care—you're right. The Stoics were full of contradictory advice. That's because different situations call for different responses.

You have to act with discretion.

Being a successful leader requires you to sort out what needs to be addressed and what needs to be ignored. Although you work in a school, it doesn't mean that you need to partake in all the daily drama. If you do, you are doomed.

Aurelius (2003) reminds us that while we have a responsibility to the people in front of us, we can choose not to let whatever they say affect us: "You don't *have* to turn this into something. It doesn't have to upset you. Things can't shape our decisions by themselves." (p. 81).

Ignore insults, ignore those who only see the bad, ignore the fact that you might not be invited to select events, and embrace the joy of missing out (JOMO). Only then can you focus on what's worth addressing.

PRACTICE TEMPERANCE

Dr. Nguyen has a habit of strolling the halls during the passing periods at his high school. He calls out to students he knows and high-fives the seniors as they walk to their next class.

One day, he's out in the hall, and the first bell rings, warning students that the passing period is almost over. As one senior is rushing to get to his next class, Dr. Nguyen sees a thick black band slide out from under the student's pant leg and onto the floor.

"Hey, wait!" he calls, stooping down to pick up the band. He's surprised to see it's an ankle monitor.

Later, he calls the student to his office and learns that the student is a recent sexual offender. He's not allowed to be near any children under 14—which is a problem because many of the freshmen on campus are that age. Not only that, but the school also has a childcare class in the building.

Dr. Nguyen calls the superintendent at once but is told that it isn't a problem. There's no other place for this kid, so he just has to "make do." Dr. Nguyen is furious.

REFLECT:

1. What temporary measures could Dr. Nguyen put in place to protect the at-risk children at his school?

2. How should Dr. Nguyen respond in the face of his supervisor's indifference?

3. What might temperance look like in this situation?

SEE THE GOOD

"When you wake up in the morning, tell yourself: the people I deal with today will be meddling, ungrateful, arrogant, dishonest, jealous, and surly. They are like this because they can't tell good from evil. But I have seen the beauty of good, and the ugliness of evil, and have recognized that the wrongdoer has a nature related to my own—not of the same blood and birth, but the same mind, and possessing a share of the divine."

- ***Marcus Aurelius*** (2003, p. 17)

Being a school administrator is one of the most rewarding careers that you could ever have. However, it's also a position that brings you into constant contact with others who have their own agendas, priorities, needs, and vendettas. At best, you may find yourself occasionally at odds with genuinely good people who are just trying their best. At worst, though, you may find yourself facing off with characters who are meddling, ungrateful, arrogant, dishonest, envious, and so much more.

No matter how hard you work, no matter how much you've turned around a school/district, no matter how much heart and intentionality you put into your decisions, you will never be able to make everyone happy.

Yet remember: You can only control *you*. No matter the circumstances, smile, be kind, and remind yourself of the main goal each day—making the staff's and students' lives better.

You always have a choice about how you react to opposition and mistakes. You can react with impatience, assigning blame to others, or you can react with patience and understanding. You'll do best to remember that you need the other people in your school. No one can be responsible for educating hundreds of students on their own! The only way this works is for everyone to work together.

To that end, be the first person to share kindness with everyone in your school/district. Be the Chief Energy Officer (CEO), and make it your personal mission to reignite the inner love and empathy that everyone has inside of them.

PRACTICE TEMPERANCE

Principal Robinson proudly walks into his newly appointed district eager to begin the new job ahead. This is a position that he has long dreamt about, and he feels extremely fortunate that the Board of Education selected him for the job.

It isn't until Robinson sets up the first administrative team meeting that some of the rumors he has heard from others outside the district start to prove true. People on his leadership team aren't talking to each other unless asked. When someone speaks, the others look down at their phones or roll their eyes, not realizing that their body language is sending up red flags. Also, one individual in this group isn't really participating at all. Robinson knows that person was another finalist for his new job.

Principal Robinson might have inherited a district in a beautiful community, but his administrative leadership team is far from a pinnacle team of teams that others would envy and try to replicate. Frustrated and stymied by the pettiness he's witnessing, he ponders what to do.

REFLECT:

1. Have you ever been in a similar situation?

2. How would you approach your new colleagues if you were in Principal Robinson's shoes?

3. How could Principal Robinson exhibit temperance and see the good in his colleagues?

ABANDON YOUR ANGER

"When you start to lose your temper, remember: There's nothing manly about rage. It's courtesy and kindness that define a human being . . . That's who possesses strength and nerves and guts, not the angry whiners. To react like that brings you closer to impassivity—and so to strength. Pain is the opposite of strength, and so is anger. Both are things we suffer from, and yield to."

• *Marcus Aurelius* (2003, p. 154)

Deep breath! Bite your tongue! How many times have you wished you'd followed such advice instead of making an emotional decision that you immediately regretted? In these moments, it's easy to see how anger is the punishment you give to yourself for somebody else's mistakes.

And being a public official creates plenty of opportunities to get angry. For instance, critics, trolls, haters, and just about anyone else in this world are likely to blame or slander you simply because they feel it's their duty to do so. You may represent a system they resent or rules they despise. You may have made a decision or enforced consequences that they feel were a personal attack. Maybe there's no reason at all.

Regardless, it's not about you; it's about them. The same people who wrote on the bathroom stalls are now writing on the internet.

Stories say that the Stoic Cato, Julius Caesar's foe and the last defender of the Roman Republic, was hit by someone in a bathhouse. Cato refused to acknowledge the incident. According to Daily Stoic (n.d.-d.), he said, "I don't even remember being hit" ("3 Stoic exercises from Cato" section).

We can learn from Cato's willful forgetfulness, his refusal to succumb to anger, and his dedication to preserving his character at all costs. Do not allow your mind to give into taunts or slander. Do not take it personally. They can "hit" you verbally and/or electronically, but true strength is found in not retaliating.

Rumors, conflict, slander, social media slights, and disrespectful emails are (or will be) regular intruders as you try to navigate your day as an administrator. Don't lose your focus on the long-term goals in favor of the short-term issues! We aren't saying you should ignore them completely, but what do you gain by losing your temper and replying harshly?

Sometimes, your anger is stirred by more commonplace and ordinary challenges: Wi-Fi and technology problems, state testing errors, cybersecurity issues, schedule miscommunications, equipment failures, and so on. But you can only control the controllables.

As a leader, you need to know when to truly sweat the small stuff and when to let it go. Don't waste your time with trivial items when the needs of the students and staff should come first.

PRACTICE TEMPERANCE

Mrs. Stuart could not be more excited to start her new administrative position within the very district that she has been a teacher in for the past seven years. As a teacher, Mrs. Stuart has always been very popular amongst most of the staff, and she has spent many hours completing extra coursework and certifications to prepare for this opportunity.

As the start date draws closer, Mrs. Stuart finds herself trying to take on both positions in hopes of making the transition smooth for the replacement teacher while trying to learn as much as possible from the outbound school leader.

In the first few weeks of her new position, things seem to be going fine, but she starts to notice some subtle changes with her colleagues. While walking down the halls one afternoon, she hears someone playing the Darth Vader theme song from Star Wars. It's funny—until she realizes that it is meant for her.

Then, on Friday, she isn't included in plans for the group happy hour. In the teacher lounge, another teacher she has always been friendly with gives her the cold shoulder when she tries to start up a personal conversation. Still, Mrs. Stuart tries to focus on the job.

PRACTICE TEMPERANCE CONT.

In month two, she finds multiple student-discipline referral slips on her desk from several of her former colleagues. She follows the student handbook, which lists the discipline policies, and decides to issue each student a warning, as she had not dealt with these students before.

The following week, Mrs. Stuart is called down to her superior's office; there are several complaints from the staff who wrote the discipline referrals. They believe that the proper discipline hasn't been issued and that she isn't maintaining the policies that support the health and safety of the staff in the building.

Mrs. Stuart feels the hot stirring of righteous indignation. Can't they see she's trying her best? Why have they abandoned her?

REFLECT:

1. Have you ever been in a similar situation as Mrs. Stuart?

2. What are the possible motivations for Mrs. Stuart's colleagues' actions?

3. What can Mrs. Stuart control in this situation?

CHAPTER 5
EQUANIMITY

stillness · calm · steadiness

"One should also be free from all disturbing emotions, not only from desire and fear, but equally from solicitude, and sensuality, and anger, that there may be serenity of mind, and that freedom from care which brings with it both evenness of temper and dignity of character."

· **Cicero** (1887, Book 2.1)

GLENN

When I was an assistant principal, I was also the supervisor for all of our homebound students—students who were sick or injured or otherwise couldn't be physically present at school. One of the girls in the program had stage-four cancer and was undergoing intensive treatments with a low likelihood of survival.

Regardless, one of our teachers was adamant that the girl complete all of the work on time, or she was going to fail her. She was also pressuring other teachers to do the same. I told the homebound teachers to focus on simply supporting this child's family and continuing to reach out with care and concern. But the other teacher continued pushing, so I finally confronted her.

"Look," I said. "If you really want to hold this child accountable, then you're going to have to personally call her mother and explain to her why you feel it's so important that her daughter complete this work while she's doing treatments."

Finally, the teacher woke up and understood how wrong she was. She stopped pushing the young girl and the other teachers. I'm grateful I was able to insist that we show up as a family and simply provide comfort and encouragement in the girl's final days.

Just six weeks later, she passed away.

PROTECT YOUR PEACE

"It is no inconsiderable matter that you have to guard; but modesty, fidelity, [p. 2152] constancy, docility, innocence, fearlessness, serenity—in short, freedom. For what will you sell these? Consider what the purchase is worth."
• **Epictetus** (1890, Book 4.3)

Buddhist monk Thích Nhất Hạnh tells a poignant story in his book, *The Heart of the Buddha's Teaching*:

> A man was rowing his boat upstream when, suddenly, he saw another boat coming toward him. He shouted, "Be careful! Be careful!" but the boat plowed right into him, nearly sinking his boat. The man became angry and began to shout, but when he looked closely, he saw that there was no one in the other boat. The boat had drifted downstream by itself. He laughed out loud. When our perceptions are correct, we feel better, but when our perceptions are not correct, they can cause us a lot of unpleasant feelings (Thích, 1998, p. 179).

From a Buddhist and Stoic point of view, wrong perceptions cause suffering. When we make assumptions about what might be happening and start looking to blame others, we give up our peace of mind. We hand over our power.

The opposite is also true. By focusing only on what is and what we can control, we can maintain peace and equanimity, our sure-footedness, and our grounding.

So the next time anything in life happens—especially a moment charged with emotion and energy—pause.

Take a breath.

Observe what is happening.

Most importantly, observe your thoughts and perceptions!

After careful observation, now you are ready to act or to speak.

PRACTICE EQUANIMITY

Miranda is the co-director for her district's ESL programs. Her partner, Jerry, suddenly starts showing up late a couple days each week, leaving her to put out whatever fires came up the prior evening. He always apologizes, mumbling something about "medical reasons," but it doesn't change the fact that she's bearing the brunt of what's supposed to be their shared responsibility.

Miranda tries to be sympathetic, but she can't help thinking he's slacking off. After one stressful morning, she finally confronts him.

"Look, Miranda," Jerry says. "I don't like talking about this, but my wife and I just started IVF. With her history of miscarriages, I promised her that I would be at every appointment and would be an active partner in the process. I told the superintendent what was going on, and he gave me permission to arrive late a couple days a week."

Miranda is stunned and ashamed. She completely misjudged him.

REFLECT:

1. How can you maintain perspective in the face of frustrating circumstances?

2. What other ways could Miranda have handled this situation? What about Jerry?

3. What strategies do you have in place for regulating your emotions?

DO NOT BE SWAYED

"To be like the rock that the waves keep crashing over. It stands unmoved and the raging of the sea falls still around it."
- **Marcus Aurelius** (2003, p. 48)

A major theme of Aurelius's *Meditations* is the reminder not to let himself be swayed, "tossed about," or manipulated like a puppet. In the Roman Empire, where senators and politicians were constantly vying for favor and influence with him, Emperor Aurelius must have been beset by near-constant requests and petitions.

And although he kept temperance in mind and endeavored to treat the people around him with dignity and respect, Aurelius was no doormat. He decided what was important to *him*—his character, his self-respect, his integrity—and lived accordingly.

No matter how others around him "raged," no matter how the waves kept crashing over him, no matter what demands were placed on his shoulders, he remained resolute in his convictions and his actions.

As a school leader, every day, you experience a version of what Aurelius did: negotiating rules, trying to meet others' needs, refereeing disagreements. It's exhausting. But you don't have to be a doormat either. You, too, can prioritize what matters most. You can be unwavering in your commitments to wisdom, justice, courage, and temperance.

PRACTICE EQUANIMITY

Rick is the top football coach in the state. He's responsible for his school's team winning five of the last seven national championships. Several players from the school who were coached by Rick have gone on to play for the top colleges in the country—and then the NFL. The community loves him; every Friday night football game is a city-wide affair.

But Principal Henry has to fire him.

Recently, one of the assistant coaches brought him evidence of Coach Rick's shady dealings: negotiating "perks" with vendors, fudging the school's rankings, and pressuring teachers to give passing grades to students who don't deserve them so that they can continue playing on the team. Principal Henry knows the backlash will be enormous. He may get fired himself. Yet it's the right thing to do.

REFLECT:

1. How can Principal Henry maintain equanimity in the face of the coming backlash?

2. Have you ever had to do something incredibly hard that you knew was right?

3. How do you stay strong in your beliefs despite resistance?

TAKE A WALK

"It does good also to take walks out of doors, that our spirits may be raised and refreshed by the open air and fresh breeze."

• **Seneca** (1900, p. 286)

When's the last time you took a 10-to-15-minute gratitude walk during the school day? When's the last time you led a walking meeting with your administrative team, teaching staff, students, or anyone? When's the last time you answered emails or made phone calls outside on a bench, at the park, on the beach, or under a tree?

It's probably been ages, maybe never! But take it from Seneca—spending time outside is a practice worth adopting. Take it upon yourself to get fresh air while walking around the school district grounds and thinking of three-to-five things you are grateful for.

Sometimes taking a few steps away from your building/district, and viewing it from a different lens can reawaken your mind to new and fresh ideas to better serve your staff, scholars, and community.

Just like you remind your teaching staff that learning doesn't just take place in the confines of four-walled classrooms, your leadership decisions don't have to be made in a stressful or stale environment.

PRACTICE EQUANIMITY

Hunter is the new technology director for a K–8 school district. For the past few weeks, he's been managing the rollout of their new Chromebooks—and it's been a disaster. Devices ending up lost or broken, parents not signing the waivers, and teachers refusing to get on board.

Optimistically, Hunter assumed everything would go well and neglected to plan for the objections and possible downfalls. So he's been working overtime for weeks trying to make up for his own bad planning, often staying late in the evening and missing lunch.

One evening, after a long day, Hunter realizes he hasn't eaten since the microwaved burrito he had the previous night for dinner.

REFLECT:

1. How do you balance working hard with taking care of yourself, even during especially busy times?

2. What are your non-negotiables for self-care?

3. How can Hunter do better going forward?

NOTHING ENDURES

"Everything that happens is either endurable or not. If it's endurable, then endure it. Stop complaining. If it's unendurable . . . then stop complaining. Your destruction will mean its end as well. Just remember: you can endure anything your mind can make endurable, by treating it as in your interest to do so. In your interest, or in your nature."

▪ *Marcus Aurelius* (2003, p. 132)

You are stronger than you think you are. Think of all of the hard things you have been through. They may have been unnecessary. They may have been unfair. But you survived. You are stronger now than you were then.

Being a leader at a school is harder now than perhaps it's ever been. You are faced with unimaginable stress, trauma, and chaos every day. You have every reason to want to leave.

You get blamed and falsely accused.

You get ignored and disregarded.

You get bullied and manipulated.

You have to make difficult decisions that the people you care about hate.

You witness heartache and devastation, and you are expected to make it better for everyone else, even when your own heart is breaking.

You could leave any day. And there's nothing necessarily wrong with leaving.

But if you don't stay, who will?

If it is within your power to change the situation, then change it. If not, ask yourself: How can I survive this with strength and dignity? How can I model fortitude and resilience for the people I serve?

Never forget the people who need you, even when they don't realize it themselves.

We all need you.

PRACTICE EQUANIMITY

Principal George is at the end of his rope. The parents, the accusations, the board meetings, the complaints, the sabotage. It's too much.

I can't do this anymore, *he thinks.*

He's been trying to fight the injustices he sees, but he constantly feels like he's alone. No one seems to care as much as he does. How does anyone survive this?

He remembers an old college friend—now the CEO of a company—who just got back from a tropical vacation. His neighbor is a hedge-fund manager who plays tennis twice a week and just remodeled his kitchen.

When was the last time George and his wife had the time and energy to upgrade something in their house?

And then he looks at a picture of his students. He sees Diego. Two years ago, George noticed Diego walking home by himself every day and learned that he was often alone for hours in the evenings because his mom works two jobs. He arranged for after-school care and personally made sure that Diego had a ride on days when his mom couldn't pick him up.

If he wasn't there, who would take care of students like Diego?

REFLECT:

1. Who are your reasons for staying in this profession?

2. What would it take to make you leave? Do you know your limits?

3. How do you endure the moments that feel unbearable so that you can relish the moments of joy?

CONCLUSION

"Just that you do the right thing.
The rest doesn't matter."
▪ Marcus Aurelius (2003, p. 69)

While writing this book, we found ourselves challenged every day to be the people Stoic philosophy trained us to be. The bickering on the school board, conflicts on our teams, bad news to be delivered, new student challenges to address—none of that stopped.

It's kind of like we've been writing this book for ourselves. And that works out pretty well since we are you.

The original Stoics have left behind many books and manuals, and new ones are being added to the list all the time. So if you've been inspired by what you've read, we encourage you to dig deeper into the philosophy. In the Appendix, we've provided a list of some of our favorite resources.

But at the end of the day, there's really just one thing to remember. One thing that we hold onto whenever we get overwhelmed or angry or anxious. One thing that keeps us grounded. One thing easy and simple enough to remember—though hard to do—when the world around us is chaotic:

Just do the right thing. The rest doesn't matter.

STOIC READING LIST

If you'd like to continue to learn more about Stoicism and read the Stoics themselves, we recommend the following books:

Meditations by Marcus Aurelius

Courage Is Calling: Fortune Favors the Brave by Ryan Holiday

Discipline Is Destiny: The Power of Self-Control by Ryan Holiday

The Obstacle Is the Way: The Timeless Art of Turning Trials into Triumph by Ryan Holiday

Ego Is the Enemy by Ryan Holiday

Stillness Is the Key by Ryan Holiday

The Lives of the Stoics by Ryan Holiday

The Tao of Seneca by Tim Ferriss

Enchiridion by Epictetus

The Art of Living: The Classic Manual on Virtue, Happiness, and Effectiveness by Epictetus, translated by Sharon Lebell

A Guide to the Good Life: The Ancient Art of Stoic Joy by William Irvine

Dying Everyday: Seneca at the Court of Nero by James Romm

How to Keep Your Cool: Seneca by James Romm

How to Be Free: Epictetus by A. A. Long

REFERENCES

Aurelius, M. (2003). *Meditations: A new translation* (G. Hays, Trans.). Modern Library.

Baldwin, J. (2007). *No name in the street*. Vintage International.

Canfield, J., & Switzer, J. (2005). *The success principles™: How to get from where you are to where you want to be*. HarperCollins Publishers.

Cicero, M. T. (1887). *On moral duties (de officiis)* (A. P. Peabody, Trans.). Little, Brown, and Company. https://oll.libertyfund.org/title/cicero-on-moral-duties-de-officiis

Daily Stoic: Ancient Wisdom for Everyday Life. (n.d.-a). *The highest good: An introduction to the 4 Stoic virtues*. https://dailystoic.com/4-stoic-virtues/

Daily Stoic: Ancient Wisdom for Everyday Life. (n.d.-b.). *Letters from a Stoic by Seneca: Book summary, key lessons and best quotes.* https://dailystoic.com/letters-from-a-stoic/

Daily Stoic: Ancient Wisdom for Everyday Life. (n.d.-c.). *8 Stoic secrets to help you build mental toughness.* https://dailystoic.com/stoic-secrets-for-mental-toughness/

Daily Stoic: Ancient Wisdom for Everyday Life. (n.d.-d.). *Who is Cato? Roman senator. Mortal enemy of Julius Caesar.* https://dailystoic.com/cato/

Epictetus. (2013). *The art of living: The classic manual on virtue, happiness, and effectiveness* (S. Lebell, Trans.). HarperOne.

Epictetus. (1890). *The works of Epictetus: His discourses, in four books, the enchiridion, and fragments* (T. Wentworth Higginson, Trans.). Thomas Nelson and Sons. https://www.perseus.tufts.edu/hopper/text?doc=Perseus%3Atext%3A1999.01.0237%3Atext%3Ddisc%3Abook%3D2%3Achapter%3D17

Heraclitus. (2003). *Fragments* (B. Haxton, Trans.). Penguin Classics.

Holiday, R. (2020). *Lives of the Stoics: The art of living from Zeno to Marcus Aurelius.* Portfolio.

Holiday, R. (2015). *The obstacle is the way: The ancient art of turning adversity to advantage.* Profile Books Ltd.

Irvine, W. B. (2008). *A guide to the good life: The ancient art of Stoic joy.* Oxford University Press.

Laertius, D. (1925). *Lives of eminent philosophers* (R. D. Hicks, Trans.). Harvard University Press. http://www.perseus.tufts.edu/hopper/text?doc=Perseus %3Atext%3A1999.01.0258%3Abook%3D7%3Achapter%3D1

National Association of Secondary School Principals. (2022, August 16). *NASSP survey of principals and students reveals the extent of challenges facing schools.* https://www.nassp.org/news/nassp-survey-of-principals-and-students-reveals-the-extent-of-challenges-facing-schools/

Powell, C. (2014). *It worked for me: In life and leadership.* Harper Perennial.

Rufus, M. (2015). *Lectures and fragments* (C. E. Lutz, Trans.). Enhanced Media Publishing.

Seneca, L. A. (1969). *Letters from a Stoic* (R. Campbell, Trans.). Penguin Classics.

Seneca, L. A. (1917). *The Tao of Seneca: Vol. 1. Practical letters from a Stoic master* (R. M. Gummere, Trans.). Loeb Classical Library. https://tim.blog/wp-content/uploads/2017/07/taoofseneca_vol1-1.pdf

Seneca, L. A. (1900). *Minor dialogues: Together with the dialogue on clemency* (A. Stewart, Trans.). George Bell and Sons. https://books.google.com/books?id=gwsvAAAAYAAJ&

Silk, D. (2015). Foreword. In J. Dollar, *Letting go of the need to be right: Experience the power of humility.* BroadStreet Publishing. https://www.google.com/books/edition/Letting_Go_of_the_Need_to_Be_Right/LneCDwAAQBAJ?hl=en&gbpv=0

Theodore Roosevelt Center. (n.d.). *The man in the arena.* Dickinson State University. https://www.theodorerooseveltcenter.org/Learn-About-TR/TR-Encyclopedia/Culture-and-Society/Man-in-the-Arena.aspx

Thích, N. H. (1998). *The heart of the Buddha's teaching: Transforming suffering into peace, joy, and liberation.* Broadway Books.

Winfrey, O. (2011, May 25). *The Oprah Winfrey Show finale.* Oprah.com. https://www.oprah.com/oprahshow/the-oprah-winfrey-show-finale_1/7

CAN WE HELP YOU DO THE RIGHT THING?

Brené Brown asks a great question that challenges all leaders:

Will you choose courage over comfort?

If we're being honest, comfort is the easy choice, and only after years of training and solid mentorship did courage become the default choice for us.

If the message in this book resonates with you and you would like help living out ancient Stoic wisdom, we humbly invite you to reach out to us and start that conversation.

We are here to serve you.

If you'd like us to come speak to your team, facilitate a workshop, coach you individually, or provide mentorship at scale, book a call with Danny at betterleadersbetterschools.com and/or contact Glenn at glennrobbins.com.

www.ingramcontent.com/pod-product-compliance
Lightning Source LLC
Chambersburg PA
CBHW070446130626
46553CB00006B/2296